Blue Crab Finds a Home

(A Book of Affirmations for Kids)

Written and Illustrated

by

Maurine Frank

CASEY –
REMEMBER... WITH
DETERMINATION YOU
CAN DO
ANYTHING!
Maurine Frank

Copyright © Maurine Frank. All Rights Reserved

ISBN: 978-1-945990-55-7

Published by High Tide Publications, Inc.
www.hightidepublications.com

Thank you for purchasing an authorized edition of *Blue Crab Finds a Home*.

High Tide's mission is to find, encourage, promote, and publish the work of authors. We are a small, woman-owned enterprise that is dedicated to the author over 50. When you buy an authorized copy, you help us to bring their work to you.

When you honor copyright law by not reproducing or scanning any part (in any form) without our written permission, you enable us to support authors, publish their work, and bring it to you to enjoy.

We thank you for supporting our authors.

Edited by Cindy L. Freeman cindy@cindylfreeman.com

Book Design by Firebellied Frog Graphic Design
www.firebelliedfrog.com

This book is dedicated

to my great-granddaughter,

Heather Maurine Frank

Blue Crab lived in the yucky mucky marsh with his mother. She told him often that he was special.

She said, "When you have *determination*, you can accomplish anything."

Blue Crab wanted to travel and see the wonders of the seashore. He also wanted to live in beautiful colored rocks.

He wondered, "How can I find **determination** and make my dreams come true?"

Blue Crab set out on his quest.

His mother told him goodbye and said, "Remember to spread joy wherever you go."

Blue Crab liked the word "joy" and he skittered along the beach saying, "I spread joy wherever I go!"

Pretty soon he met a seagull named Gully. "I love seeing you so happy," Gully said. "It makes me happy too!"

Blue Crab said, "I am looking for determination."

Gully did not know what **determination** was, but he said, "I hope on your quest you will remember to tell yourself that you can do whatever you set your mind to do."

Then Blue Crab came across a little turtle that had fallen off a log. He was struggling, but he couldn't manage to turn himself upright.

Blue Crab flipped him over. Tommy Turtle said, "You are truly a good friend, and I thank you for your kindness."

Blue Crab told Tommy about his quest. Tommy Turtle said, "You care about others and treat them with kindness. I think you might find determination along the way."

Blue Crab's mind was set on finding *determination*, as well as some beautiful colored rocks. But his quest wasn't going well. He was starting to feel sad.

Just then he spotted a beautiful, colorful butterfly named Flit. Flit noticed Blue Crab was having a sad day.

"Don't be sad," he said. "Turn that frown upside down because if you look for it, you'll always find a reason to smile."

Blue Crab explained he was on a quest. He told Flit about meeting Gully and Tommy, but he needed to find determination and that wasn't going too well. He said, "I can't stay because I need to keep searching. This is important."

Flit said, "You must be very special to be brave enough to leave the yucky mucky marsh. Also, how wonderful of you to spread joy as you go because that is so important. You have made the seashore a better place by being kind and a good friend to others. These are reasons to smile your biggest smile. Most of all, don't you see that since you've not given up your quest, you've had determination all along?"

Blue Crab's mood was immediately lifted. He realized he had *determination* after all!

He thanked Flit, waved goodbye, and skittered on down the beach as he repeated...

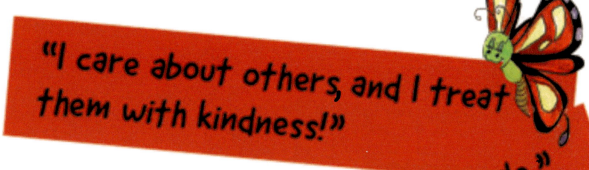

As he said these things over and over, Blue Crab realized he had a big smile on his face, and he was not sad any more.

Just then he came around a bend in the beach and there in front of him was...

a big pile of the most beautiful colored rocks he had ever seen!

THE END!

I hope you will always remember the things Blue Crab learned as he was finding determination.

1. I am special!

2. I spread joy wherever I go!

3. I am a good friend to everyone.

4. I care about others, and I treat them with kindness!

5. There is always a reason to smile!

6. With determination, I can do anything."

About the Author and Illustrator

Maurine Frank is an artist and retired Leadership Development Consultant and lover of children. Her educational background is psychology, and her professional years were focused on team effectiveness and writing training and development programs, which has resulted in a background of writing inspirational and encouragement articles.

Her art is drawn from the beautiful seaside landscapes where she lives in Mathews, Virginia, and it's only natural that her first book takes place on a beautiful beach.

I know that every individual is significant and believe that our existence affects countless people in countless ways. I also believe that within each of us is a spark that can be extinguished or can glow based on encouragement from others. I'm convinced that taking pride in our light and using it for good is essential and it begins at an early age.

This book is dedicated to Heather Maurine Frank, my great-granddaughter and namesake. I want her exposed to encouraging, positive books about the impact of kindness on others. Since she is three, these books must be colorful and engaging, with a lively, fun character to hold her interest. I've been writing and developing team-effectiveness programs for most of my career. The heart of this work is similar to writing a children's story with a solid moral The moral in Blue Crab Finds a Home is if you care about others and treat them with kindness, you will bring joy into people's lives and ultimately be supported in doing whatever you put your mind to.

Made in the USA
Middletown, DE
14 July 2022